QUICK WAYS TO BE A GOOD LEADER

24 Tips to Manage Better and Lead Well

Other Titles By Karl Bimshas

"So, I've Been Thinking"

"Leaders Don't Shrug"

"GO GET IT!"

"Pushing Back the Ocean"

"How to Stay When You Want to Quit"

"Disposable Journal"

"Write Advice"

"Perspectives"

QUICK WAYS TO BE A GOOD LEADER

24 Tips to Manage Better and Lead Well

Karl Bimshas

BimMedia

San Diego, California

First Printing 2018

Karl Bimshas Consulting
7676 Hazard Center Drive, Suite 500
San Diego, CA 92108

www.KarlBimshasConsulting.com

Photo credit: Katiana Bimshas

ISBN: 978-0-359-15812-6

DEDICATION

For Katiana and Jonas. Two natural leaders who are not afraid to regularly improve themselves.

TABLE OF CONTENTS

INTRODUCTION

You can pick up dozens of books that will tell you what makes a good leader. When you are brand new to leadership, you might try to read all of them. You may be trying to combat imposter syndrome, or you may have the conscientiousness to study and learn so, you don't screw up. That is admirable, particularly in light of the findings that nearly 60% of new managers fail within the first 18-24 months in their role. By deciding you want to be a good leader, instead of a lousy one, you significantly enhance your odds of success.

Effective management and leadership can be difficult. There are days (and nights) when external motivation or internal inspiration is lacking, and you feel directionless. That is not a luxury you can afford if you are serious about being a professional who can be counted on to manage better and lead well.

In this brief guide, you will learn 24 tips that enhance the qualities of a good leader. Use them as a daily reminder, or turn them into an action plan for a month's worth of leadership development.

Refer to these tips often, and you will have a head start managing better and leading well.

Tip 1

MAKE DECISIONS

To move forward; leaders make decisions. Today, make and act on one big decision you have been putting off. Simple, but not always easy.

TIP #2

INSPIRE CREATIVITY

There is joy in solving problems and finding solutions. There is a pain in letting things rot, fester or stagnate. As a leader, you set the stage; which one do you prefer. Feed yourself with something that inspires you today, and then encourage creativity in others. (Repeat often.)

TIP #3

BE ACCOUNTABLE FOR YOUR ACTIONS

Good leaders are not situationally responsible. When you goof, you own it. When you succeed, you share the credit. That is the compact if you want to be taken seriously. Pick an important item you are wavering on and find someone to hold you accountable for the results.

TIP #4

COMMUNICATE
EXPECTATIONS

Whim is difficult to anticipate. People do not always know what's going on in their leader's head. Thinking does not make it so. Acting on those thoughts does. Be clear about what you want. If people do not understand you, that is on you - not them.

TIP #5

BE DEEPLY CURIOUS

The arrogant think they have all the answers. Leaders know when they do not and ask better questions. Pick one assumption you have that you are sure of, and then look for ways to prove yourself wrong.

TIP #6

PROBLEM SOLVE

Leaders work on solving problems. Sometimes that involves creating new ones, which is okay. Solve those too. Make a list of all the current issues that are on your plate. Eliminate the ones that you have no control or impact on, e.g., the weather. Choose the problem that when solved, would positively impact other problems too. This problem is now one of your goals. Put a singular focus on solving it. After it is resolved, celebrate and go find another.

TIP #7

FREQUENTLY COMMUNICATE

As a leader, you often get great ideas. Also, remember to reinforce your existing vision, mission, values, etc. You might think you are repeating yourself. It's okay. What you think is essential bears repeating. Incorporate new feedback and stay on message.

TIP #8

EMBRACE AND MANAGE CHANGE

Leadership thrives on change; management too frequently does not. Instead of dreading inevitable change, pay attention, find the predictable elements that you can control, and approach the rest with curiosity.

TIP #9

VALUE CUSTOMERS AND END USERS

Everyone has customers or end users, the person who benefits from your work. Without them, you do not have much work. Do you serve them begrudgingly, or with a sincere smile? Leaders who value client relationships are responsive, inquisitive, helpful, and grateful. See if you can be all four with each client you interact with today.

TIP #10

ENJOY YOUR ROLE

You will not love all of it, but you had better love most of it. Think about your role as a leader and list the elements you dislike against the items you enjoy. If you find you lack gratification and joy the majority of the time, how capable of a leader do you think you are? Today, overcompensate and pursue the tasks that fulfill you.

TIP # 11

SHARE A VISION

Where do you want to go? What can you see that others do not ... yet? It is one thing to see in your mind's eye where you want to go, what you want to create and achieve. To get there as a leader, you will have to share your vision with others who can help. To do that, make it a sensible vision. That means two things. It should be currently out of reach, but not out of the realm of possibility. Second, you should describe it in a way that invokes all of the senses.

TIP #12

BEHAVE ETHICALLY

If you find it difficult to operate within the rules, you might not be cut out for leadership. Make sure you are acting congruently with your morals, values, and ethics.

TIP #13

GIVE CREDIT AND TAKE BLAME

Leadership is finding the nuance between, "It's not about you." and "You are 100% responsible." When you receive praise, say thank you, and if anyone helped you achieve something, thank them. When you receive blame, accept the feedback and fix the problem.

TIP # 14

FOCUS ON A GOAL

Wishing is not enough. Consistent active participation makes dreams come true. As a leader, you had better be goal driven, and that goal or those goals should bring you closer to your vision. Keep yourself, and others focused on the things that do that, and away from distractions.

TIP #15

GET BETTER AT SETTING GOALS

Don't confuse goals with wishes. Goals are not easy. It takes much effort to set a goal for yourself or others. You cannot merely command a goal into being. Secondly, good goals are motivating and specific. Vague goals get vague results. Sometimes you announce your goals, and sometimes you keep them close to your vest. Whom you share them with matters. How and how often you measure progress matters. How you celebrate along the way matters. No goal, no direction. No direction, no point. Always have a great goal.

TIP #16

PAY ATTENTION TO YOUR PERSONAL DASHBOARD

When you manage and lead others, it is easy to get engrossed with their performance and metrics. Pay attention to YOUR personal dashboard as well. Not only business results, but also improvements in your relationships, health, education, etc. should get your attention. Measure the important aspects of your life. Knowing your measures is the only way you can maintain and improve your performance.

TIP #17

TAKE THE INITIATIVE

There are those who wait for someone else to act, and there are those who will not wait, and instead make things happen. Don't wait to see who moves first, be the person who moves first.

TIP #18

SET YOUR OWN EXAMPLE

When you admonish people for acting a certain way, and then you act that way, you look foolish. Today, and every day after, don't think you can just set the example and consider your job to be done. You have to also BE your own example.

TIP #19

MEASURE THE RIGHT THINGS CONSISTENTLY OVER TIME

Anything can be measured; however, this does not mean everything should be measured. Pick the items (units, calls, dollars, scores, errors, etc.) that are most relevant to your important goal(s) and track them over time (every hour, day, week) without fail. Don't miss a measurement. Be consistent. Fix your attention on your leading indicators to influence your lagging indicators. Don't change the goal post if you do not like the trend or results. Look for what's working. Celebrate successes and keep the trend line moving in the direction you seek.

TIP #20

POSSESS A POSITIVE ATTITUDE

Your attitude colors and filters everything you pull in and push out, and it is one of the rare things you have complete control over. Today, lead from a positive place. Find the best in people and give the best of yourself.

TIP #21

VALUE RELATIONSHIPS

You are a reflection of your closest relationships. It is easy to take advantage of your meaningful relationships. It is easy to take shortcuts and leave them shortchanged. Stop doing that. Make a plan and a commitment to showing people how much you value them.

TIP # 22

BUILD A RECORD OF SUCCESS

Action breeds action. Make a note of your accomplishments, not to humble brag, to record where you have been and what you have done. If you have been doing that, trends of strengths and weaknesses will appear. Make adjustments when starting your next endeavor.

TIP #23

BE FLEXIBLE AS CONDITIONS CHANGE

Stability is nice; change is inevitable. Learn to discern when to be unyielding, and when to go with the flow. A river follows the same basic route but is in constant movement.

TIP #24

POSSESS COURAGE

Make a distinction between danger and fear. Avoid danger and confront fear. Confront something that fills you with dread. Confidence grows out of competence, which you achieve by doing. Help to destroy a fear today, either yours or someone else's.

This is your baseline measure. It's subjective, but how you feel after reviewing your answers will give you a lot of information on your current state of happiness and how much energy you will need to devote to improving your outlook.

FINAL THOUGHTS

These 24 tips were aimed at helping you to pay attention to the essential leadership skills that often get lost over time. The leadership qualities outlined can apply to any level of leadership in any discipline.

The intention was to help inspire you to maximize your existing strengths and continuously improve yourself and your organization by using the powers of vision, passion, and action.

The rest is up to you. Leaders take on more significant responsibilities, and sometimes burdens than they originally signed up for. If you are going to lead, meet that challenge and lead well.

About the Author

Karl Bimshas, Boston-bred and California-chilled leadership consultant and author of several books and programs designed for busy professionals who want to manage better and lead well.

With an M.S. in Executive Leadership from the University of San Diego and a B.A. in Mass Communications from Emerson College in Boston, Karl Bimshas has held operational and sales leadership positions in public and private corporations. As a sought-after executive coach and leadership consultant, he's helped busy professionals find, set and get their great goals by discovering the a-ha within.

Want help being a better leader in your organization?

Karl Bimshas Consulting is the leadership development and accountability firm that busy professionals turn to help grow their confidence and support around management and leadership.

For more information, visit
www.KarlBimshasConsulting.com
or call 619-497-2670

www.ingramcontent.com/pod-product-compliance
Lightning Source LLC
Chambersburg PA
CBHW021026180526
45163CB00005B/2131